THE EYE OF THE HEART

THE VISIONARY ART AND SYMBOLS OF NEIL HAGUE

'The brilliant and inspired symbolic art of one of the world's most unique and individual artists.'
David Icke

CW00433726

The artwork in this book of postcards spans several years soley driven by my passion for the 'truth vibrations'. The book is a 'snapshot' of the 'many images' I have been producing independently or commissioned to do so over the past few years. They 'illuminate' the words of the author, David Icke and in many ways this book is dedicated to him and his monumental work.

As an illustrator my work attempts to focus the viewer on inner states of awareness, to console and speak of higher levels of consciousness. I use 'symbols' as a vehicle for creating a resonance with *consciousness*. Therefore 'alchemy' and 'art' go hand in hand, and the paintings here intend to both celebrate and inform, to illustrate and 'illuminate', through the wonder and magnificence of the human soul. Of course some of my imagery will show the 'shadow side', not least through the images that have been used to illustrate the 'occult elite power structures' and their puppeteers that have instigated anything but peace on earth.

As I compile this project, war has been 'waged' *on* Libya, just one more war instigated by the 'lords of war'. The assault on Libya won't be the last unless we 'wake up' and 'see' what is *truly* happening to our world. War is 'profitable' on many levels to those that instigate such horror. Elite 'energy vampires' (that feed on us) *demand* a 'perpetual' war on Earth. Therefore our *global* economies (and taxation) have been inextricably linked to war throughout history, with income taxes rising to 50% by 1945 and continued to grow to 80% by the mid 1960's! World Wars and the taxation that the 'elite' ultimately demand will continue to blight humanity, unless we refuse to participate with the injustice and 'madness' of both the 'military-industrial complex' and the 'economics' that support war. A declaration of a 'State of Peace' would be to 'refuse to participate' in the economics (the world over) that provide governments with the means to both start and maintain wars!

Peace on earth comes from peace within - all war is sick!

Those that support war too often hardly stop to reflect beyond the polarity of the situation, to see the devastation such action brings to all life. Wars are started through 'acts of violence' and those that want to bring about war to suit their own agenda - a Global Fascist State! Too often these 'acts' lead to multiple theatres of war (by grand design). The world economy thrives off war, *without war there would be peace on Earth!* All war is 'in-humane' no matter what the rhyme or reason for it! In the face of such 'devastation' we need to *remember* our *true* human creative power. My art, like *all* art, is an acknowledgement of the true creative potential within us. It's our own unique *vibration*. As creators we have a plentitude and magnitude of 'magic and power' at our disposal. Instead of focusing on 'acts of destruction', 'mind games' and endless 'fears' projected through the media, our governments and the controlling 'forces' that drain our spirits, we need to summon the 'infinite' creative power within us. We *are* magic at our *core* (our 'eye of the heart') and this power is greater than any army when we focus our intention for truth and peace. Acts of war, both 'inner and outer', are a failure to embrace, contemplate and consider our actions in relation to others. As Ralph Waldo Emerson said, "Nothing can bring you peace but yourself."

Art for peace

The true power of peace is 'consciousness' over 'thinking', or 'wisdom' over 'intellect'. My art has been an attempt to 'speak' to 'consciousness' rather than the intellect and to honor a truth that we are all *one* when we act out of *consciousness* and *oneness*. My image of the *Earth-Mind Prison,* created as an alternative cover image for *Human Race Get Off Your Knees,* attempts to portray this idea. It shows how the 'mind' can become a 'battlefield' of doubt and fear, or a *'prison'* built through the 'intellect' and rational (left brained) 'logic'. It's a place where the creative imagination hardly ever gets to visit or reside. By using *our* creative imagination, we are 'reminded' of *our* own power and uniqueness as *creators*. With this knowledge we then carry a responsibility as 'human beings' to 'care take', to 'nurture' and to protect our future generations. Even in the face of global adversity and strife, we still have a responsibility to support, aid and celebrate life. True human power is one that acts out of 'compassion' and 'love' for others. In truth 'acts of war' are 'acts of fear', they are 'reactions' and therefore 'mindless' by definition. In this context my art speaks of 'power symbols' that are intricately connected to our 'consciousness' and the 'wisdom' that extends beyond 'body and mind'. It is through our creative power, therefore, that we can change *our* reality.

Placing the stone in the tree

In my vision the power of 'true human creativity' and the 'truth vibrations' are symbolised as a great celestial tree that stands firmly connected to the Earth. In truth, it is also a symbol of the Earth with its branches or arms reaching into the infinite Universe. The 'sacred tree' offers both *shelter* and *protection* to *all life*, it is a 'harbinger' of 'otherworlds'. The tree is also symbolic of the 'brain' and the multiple inner worlds of human perception. The 'trunk' (in my image) is the spinal column, that sits below the 'earth-brain' (the tree) converging at the seat of our 'true sight'. The two halves of the brain symbolise both the Earth 'maze' and 'labyrinth' as shown on my cover painting for the book by David Icke: *Re-*

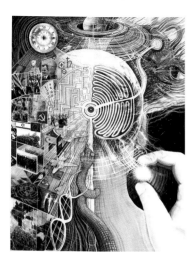

member Who You Are. The *left* side of the brain is the maze of logical confusion, a projection (a holographic matrix) that is anchored by the Moon. It 'covets' our 'third eye' and is symbolic of the world we live in – a world of *'Moonopoly'*. The Labyrinth is a similar construct that offers a way into the underworld or the inner-worlds of the mind. The *right* side of the brain is the part of the tree that connects us to 'infinite worlds of possibility'. It is the place of 'intuition' and 'imagination' *fired* by the Sun and the 'solar plasma' energies that *create* the Universe. The tree is also a symbol of the 'breath of life' and like the upside down trees of our lungs (bronchioles) this symbol is one of sustenance, co-existence and 'life' itself. It is also a symbol of reverence for the silent spaces between our thoughts, our breath, and the 'stilling' of our mind. The brain or sacred tree is the 'inner temple', and like all places of worship from the 'forest groves' to the 'cathedral', it is a place

where we can *go within* to attain inner peace. The 'placing' of the stone in the 'tree of life', at the centre of the earth-brain, is a symbol for the *remembering* of who we truly are. The hand of the human divine form places the stone (the 'star of truth') in its rightful place - in the centre. In doing so it illuminates the pineal gland and opens our 'true sight', our infinite *awareness*. The placing of the crystal stone, that carries the 'truth vibration', begins the process of 'remembering' and 'seeing' the world for what it truly is! In my vision, the 'knowing' and 'feeling' of our truth, brings about the 'end' of the false reality (the matrix projection), which is merely a vibrationary prison that is imposed on the 'many' by the 'few'. We are all 'earth stars' with jail break in our hearts - freedom calls!

Symbols of sun, moon and lion consciousness

Much of my art weaves together symbols of my personal journey, attempting to utilise the creative imagination and to celebrate the magic and the mystery in all life. As an artist I am interested in the 'truth'– nothing else will do!
Symbols relating to the Sun, the Earth, 'Saturn' and the Moon can be found at the core of human perception, in fact they 'control' our perception more than we are aware! We live in a false reality of 'X' Factors', a *place* where the 'movie projection' *shapes* our reality. Becoming conscious of how symbols (sacred shapes) effect us, has been paramount to my work. By painting ancient symbols, I have given life to them within this reality, and I have also purposefully reversed their power at times. The image of the lion on David's book cover in recent years was created with this reversed knowledge in mind. Rather than a 'ruling' force to be fearful of, it has become a symbol of

the *collective* spirit and courage that humanity will bring to the *world* to denounce the 'false priesthoods' that have spent thousands of years working to enslave humanity.

The image on the left called *Here Comes the Moon,* I painted in London in 1993. It was one of several 'channelled' paintings originally turned into a postcard that helped connect me with David Icke all of those years ago. Here the Moon is being 'blown' by a devil, a symbol of Satan, towards the Earth in ancient times; while the great 'eye' watches over this manoeuvre. The 'all-seeing eye' I now see as a symbol of *Saturn* and therefore the subject was as relevant then as it is now, when I consider my recent work. The lion on the cover of my book *Kokoro,* which also means 'heart', was based on how I see myself outside of this illusion. The many lion images I have made were painted with the knowledge that the lion *cannot* be enslaved and through this 'true' power we become sovereign human beings! We are the Imagi-*nation,* a 'new nation' of 'lion-people' in the making that have seen beyond the veil.

The human imagination is the key to unlock the door marked 'infinite awareness'. Becoming conscious human beings, we can then enter that 'State of Peace'. To achieve peace for ourselves, and for the world, we must first accept some kind of 'change' in

our thoughts and imagination of ourselves. As Gandhi said, "We must become the change we wish to see in the world".

Through my art and illustrations over the past 20 years I have attempted to capture the 'great awakening' that is *of our time*. I have also wanted to 'illuminate' the 'changes' that *are happening* because of the 'truth vibrations'. The work here is a selection of both old and new imagery, and bears testimony to the hidden knowledge that is now passing in front of our eyes! It is time to 'open' our eyes further and see *all* that there is to *see*. It is also a time for the *'eye of the heart'*, the *core of our being*, to become a beacon of light and truth. My vision through my art is designed to aid the viewer in this task. The 'eye of the heart' is the 'place' where we 'create' and 'focus' our unique vibration, so to effect a change in our reality. I have dedicated my life's work to this new way of seeing and I hope you will get something from the cards and images here too. As Clarissa Pinkola Estes said, "One of the most calming and powerful actions you can do to intervene in a stormy world is to stand up and show your soul."

Peace be with you
Neil Hague

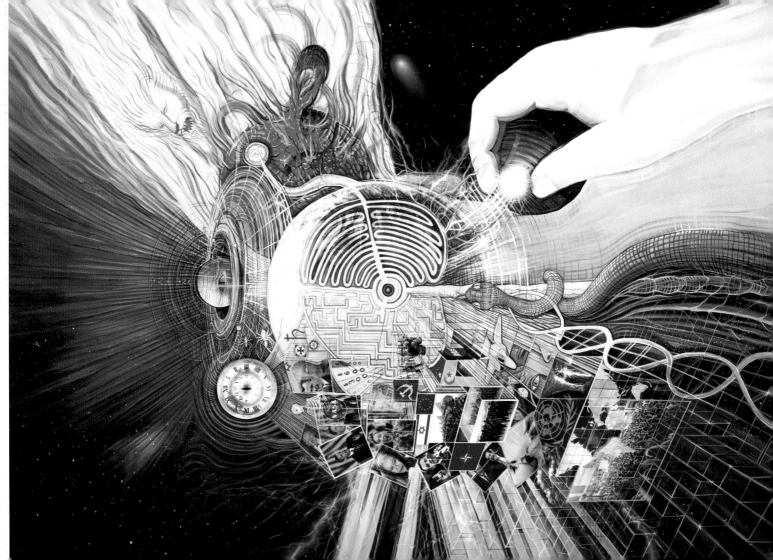

'When you see the clouds moving from the east, you say the
rain is coming and it is. When the desert wind blows, you say
it will be hot and it its.
All of you can read the signs of the Earth and the sky,
Why is it you can't read the signs of the time?
The Kingdom of Heaven is here, now!'

Luke 12: 54

PLACING THE STONE IN THE TREE - ENDING THE FALSE PROJECTION
© NEIL HAGUE 2012 ★ DAVID ICKE BOOKS LTD

WWW.NEILHAGUE.COM

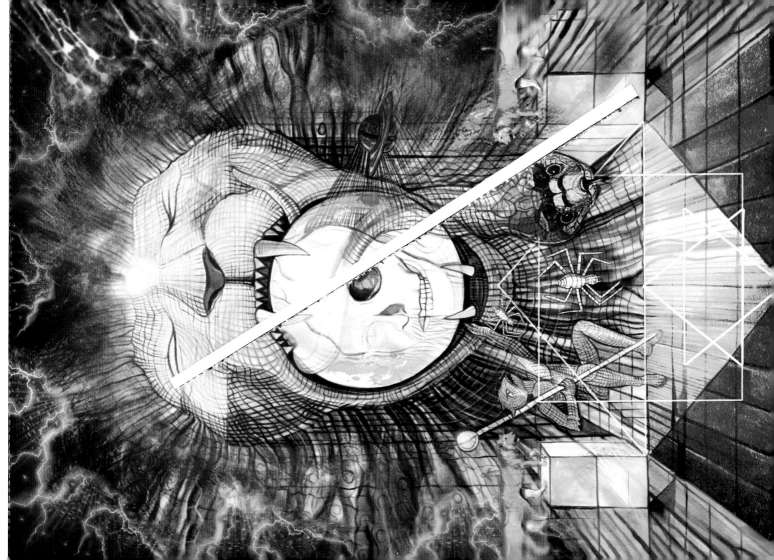

In one night the Atlantic Continent was caught up with the Moon, And became an opaque Globe far distant clad with moony beams. The visions of Eternity, by reason of narrowed perceptions, are become weak visions of time and space, fixed into furrows of death: Til deep dissimulation is the only defence an honest man has left...

William Blake - *Jerusalem*. plate 49

WWW.NEILHAGUE.COM

The moon is rightly believed to be the star of the spirit that saturates the earth and fills bodies by its approach and empties them by its departure. The blood even of humans increases and diminishes with its light and leaves and herbage are sensitive to it... the Moon penetrates into all things.

Pliny *(Allegro)*

*Sin (Akkadian: Su'en, Sîn) or Nanna (Sumerian: DŠEŠ.KI, DNANNA) was the god of the moon in Mesopotamian mythology.

WWW.NEILHAGUE.COM

'When you are constantly moving forward,
searching for the cutting edge,
everyone behind you always believes you have gone too far.

The further back from the cutting edge they are,
the more extreme, and indeed insane,
you appear to them, to be.

In this way, one person's "madness"
can be another's commonsense.'

David Icke

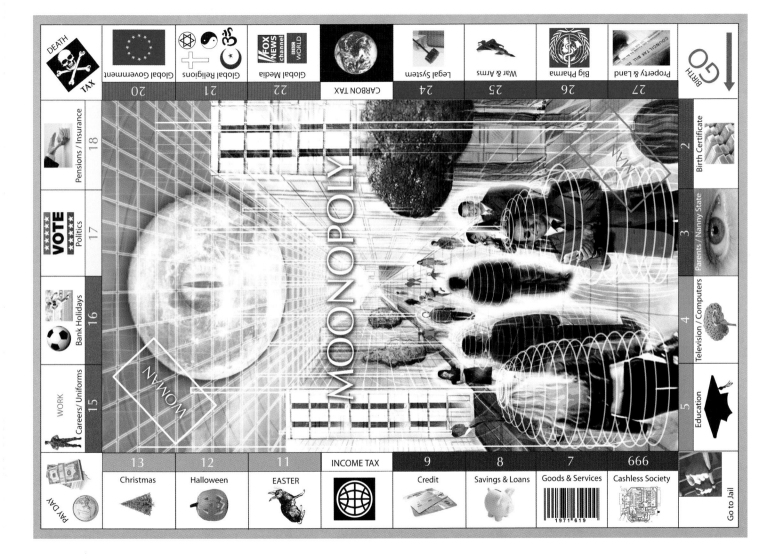

'All movements, actions, and manifestations of people, animals, and plants depend upon the moon and are controlled by the moon... The mechanical part of our life depends upon the moon, is subject to the moon. If we develop in ourselves consciousness and will, and subject our mechanical life and all our mechanical manifestations to them, we shall escape from the power of the moon.'

G. I. Gurdjieff 1916

WWW.NEILHAGUE.COM

The first peace, which is the most important, is that which comes within the souls of people when they realize their relationship, their oneness, with the universe and all its powers, and when they realize that at the center of the universe dwells the Great Spirit, ...and that this center is really everywhere, it is within each of us.

Black Elk

WWW.NEILHAGUE.COM

'Woe to you scribes and Pharisees hypocrites all. You shut out the Kingdom of heaven from man, you don't go in yourselves, nor do you let anyone else enter.

You bow before the letter of the law but violate the very heart of the law.

You are like whited sepulchres, all clean and pristine on the outside, but on the inside full of dead men's bones and all corruption.

Yours is the house of desolation, the home of the lizard and the spider, how can any of you escape damnation.'

Mathew 23: 13-39
Attributed to Jesus (taken from Franco Zeffirelli's Jesus of Nazareth)

'Sometimes it's hard to know, which way you're supposed to go. But deep inside you know you're strong, if you follow your heart you can't be wrong. Stand up! (stand up) for what is right, Be brave and get ready to fight. Hold on! (hold on) we're friends for life. And ...if we come together as one, complete the quest that we've begun. We will win the battle...'

Galactic Battle Pokemon

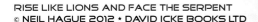

RISE LIKE LIONS AND FACE THE SERPENT
© NEIL HAGUE 2012 ★ DAVID ICKE BOOKS LTD

WWW.NEILHAGUE.COM

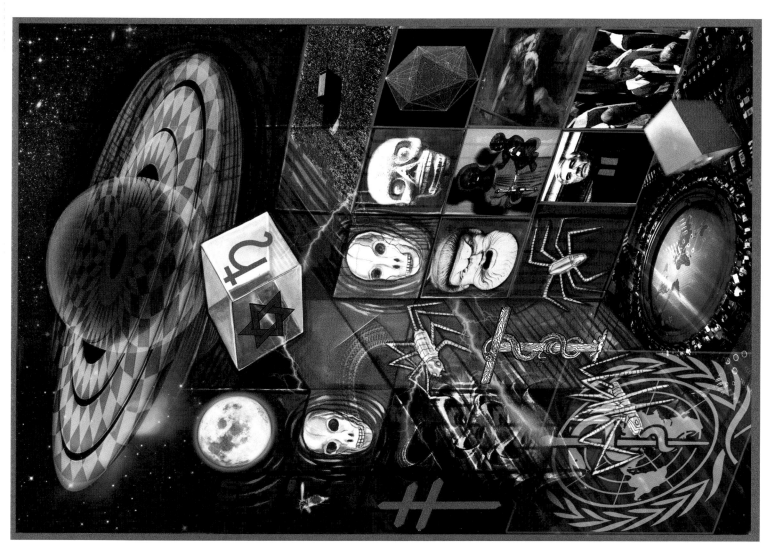

'One Ring to rule them all,
One Ring to find them,
One Ring to bring them all
and in the darkness bind them.'

J. R. R. Tolkien
The Fellowship of the Ring

'Man cannot discover new oceans unless he has the courage to
lose sight of the shore.'

Andre Gide

WWW.NEILHAGUE.COM

'God appears and god is light
To those poor souls who dwell in night
But does a human form display
To those who dwell in realms of day.'

William Blake